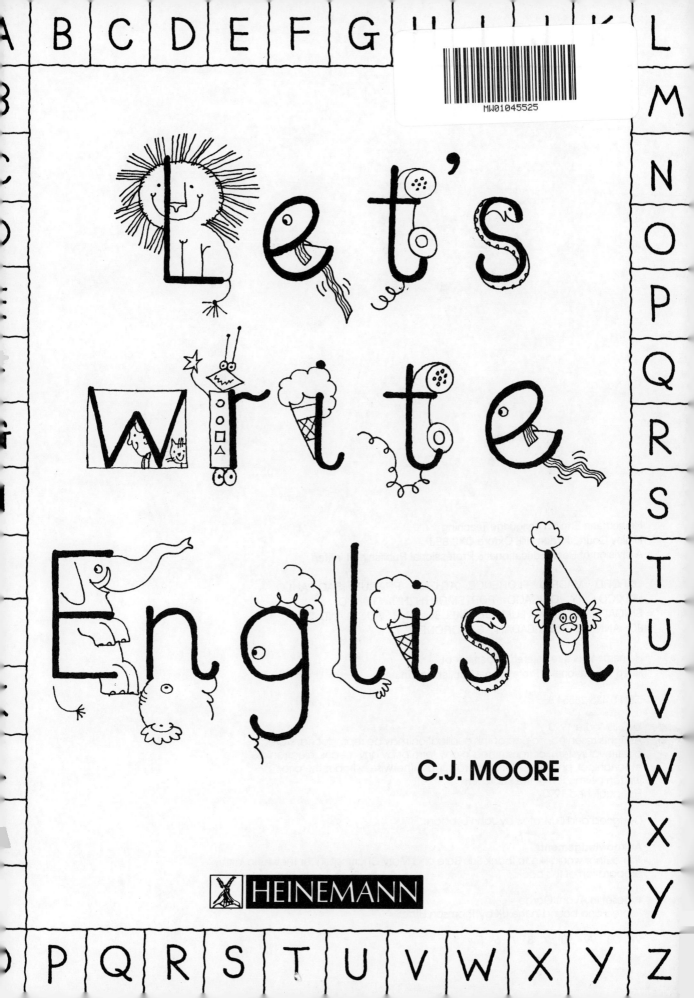

Let's write English

C.J. MOORE

HEINEMANN

Heinemann English Language Teaching
Halley Court, Jordan Hill, Oxford OX2 8EJ
A division of Reed Educational & Professional Publishing Limited

OXFORD MADRID FLORENCE ATHENS PRAGUE SÃO PAULO
MEXICO CITY CHICAGO PORTSMOUTH (NH) TOKYO
SINGAPORE KUALA LUMPUR MELBOURNE AUCKLAND
JOHANNESBURG IBADAN GABORONE

Heinemann is a registered trademark of
Reed Educational & Professional Publishing Limited

ISBN 0 435 28554 8

Designed and illustrated by John Lobban

Acknowledgements
The author would like to thank Sue Bale and Mary Charrington for their help in the
preparation of this book.

Typeset in Avant Garde
Printed and bound in the UK by Thomson Litho

97 98 99 10 9 8 7 6 5

Contents

To the teacher

General Introduction

Let's write English is a basic introduction to the English alphabet and numbers. It teaches letter formation but not joined-up writing. Pupils are introduced letter-by-letter to the alphabet in both upper and lower case. The written formation of each letter is then practised. Varied writing activities, including games and puzzles, are provided. Numbers one to ten, in figures and words, are covered after the alphabet. Finally activity rhymes or chants which help to reinforce the sounds of English letters are given in a separate *Say and do* section. By the end of the course, pupils should be ready to start with confidence a main English course such as JACARANDA.

Starting to write

First see that each pupil is equipped with a well-sharpened pencil (HB) and a clean rubber. Teach the correct way to hold a pencil. Pictures of right-handed and left-handed children holding pencils are shown on page 62.

Writing exercises should be done slowly and carefully as they are an important preparation for good handwriting. The exercises will teach control over position and size. Pupils who rush at the exercises will not benefit. Teach care and accuracy at this stage.

Do one exercise at a time, demonstrating clearly on the blackboard what the pupil should do. A completed example with arrows is given for each letter on the top right-hand corner of the page.

Pupils will enjoy colouring the pictures when they have finished an exercise. Tracing over the exercises on tracing paper is valuable extra practice.

a is for

arm

athlete

Write

a a

a a

A A

Ring the a's

@bracadabra

Finish and colour

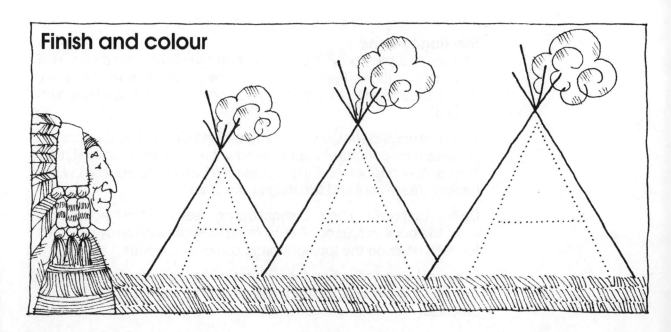

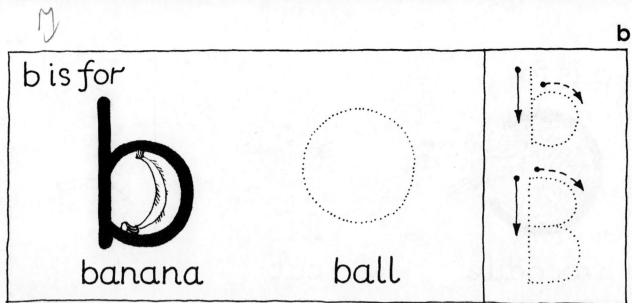

b is for

banana   ball

Write

b b

b b

B B

Ring the b's

badbadbadbadbad

Complete the words

_all   _ag   _us   _oy

c

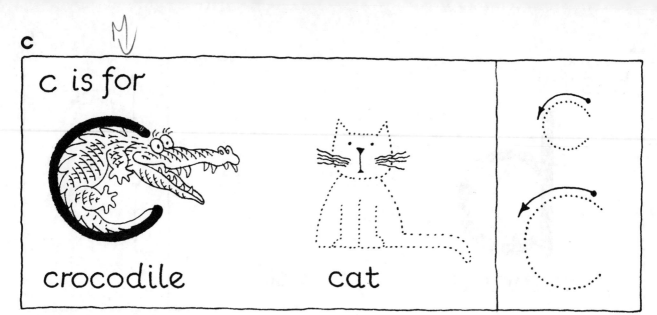

c is for

crocodile   cat

Write

c   c

c   c

c   c

Ring the word

cat   t a d a t c a r c a t d a b c a r

car   r a c c a t d a r c a r b a t a r

cap   p a t a c a b c a p r b c a r c a n

cow   w o b a c o w d o w a o w b o w

cup   a g o c u p l b a p u p g n p a

4

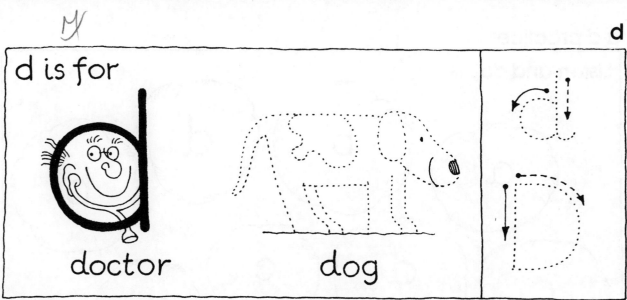

d is for

doctor

dog

Write

d d

d d

D D

Join the d's

a	d	b	a	a	b	a	b	d	a	d	b	d	a	b
d	a	d	b	d	a	b	d	b	d	a	d	b	d	d
b	b	a	d	b	d	d	a	a	b	b	a	a	b	a

Complete the words

desk   _oor   _og   _ish

a-d practice

Listen and do

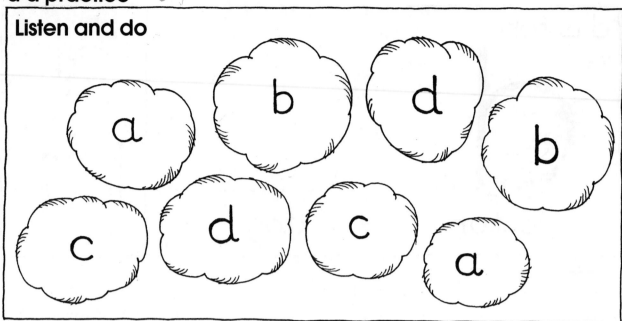

Listen and write

....
....
_____
....
_____

Find the letters

6

Say the letters

D B A C B D C A D

a d a b c d a b c

Join the letters

A B C D B A C D C B A D

c d b a c d b a d a b c

Write

A   a

B   b

C   c

D   d

Mend the wall

e   *Miguel*

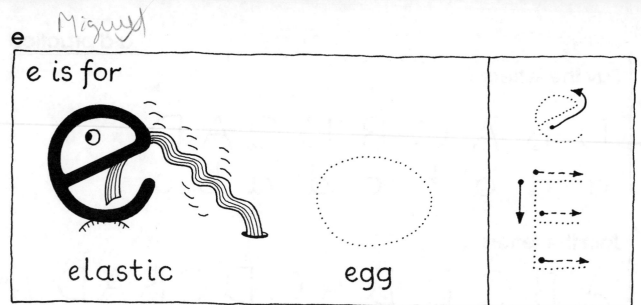

e is for

elastic   egg

Write

e ℯ

e ℯ

E E

Ring the odd one out

a a a a a ⓒ a a a   c c e c c c c c

B B B B B B B E   E E A E E E E E

Join the *e*'s.
Draw an egg

c a c a c   c   a e a e a
a c c c   e   e   e   e a c a
a c c e   c   a e c c
a c c e   a e a c c
c a a c e   a   a e a c c
c a c c e   c   e c a c
a a c e   e   e a c c
c c a c   c c a c

8

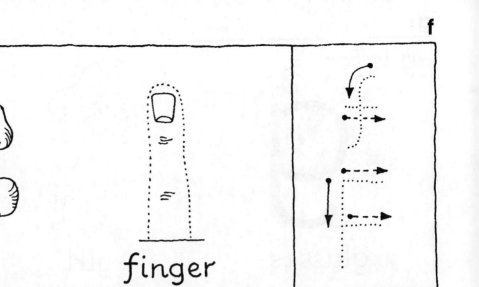

f is for

fruit

finger

Write

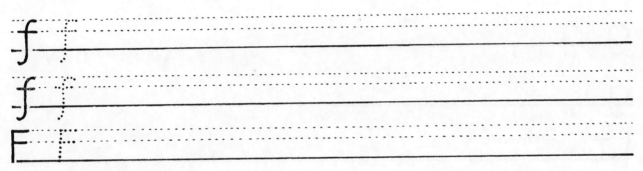

f

f

F

Ring the word

face	efac	faec	(face)	feac
fruit	ruitf	itfru	truif	fruit
foot	toof	foot	foto	tofo
fish	ifsh	hifs	hisf	fish

Colour the fish and the frog

g

g is for

glasses

girl

Write

g   g

g   g

G   G

Complete the words

ba g

le_

e_ _

do_

Write

badge

10

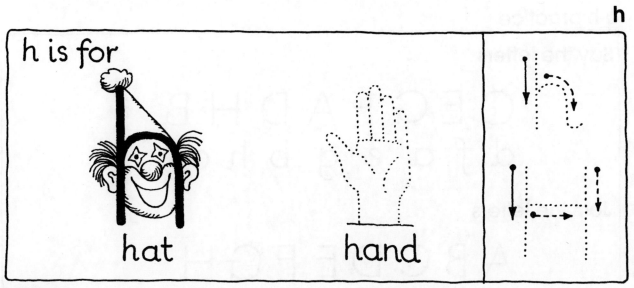

h is for

hat

hand

Write

h h

h h

H h

Complete and join

head

_air

_at

_and

a-h practice

Say the letters

C E G F A D H B

d f a e g b h c

Join the letters

A B C D E F G H

d e h b a g c f

Write

E .... e

F .... f

G .... g

H .... h

Spell these words

face   cage   bag   head   badge

Listen and do

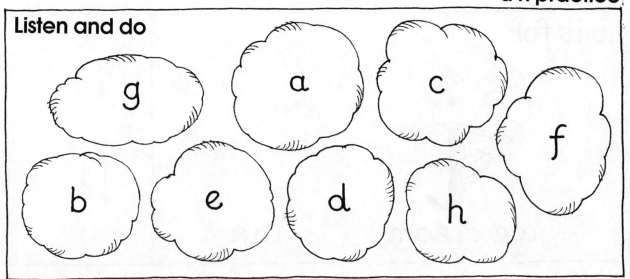

Listen and write

....
....

....
....

Find the letters

i is for

ice cream   ink

Write

i

i

i

Complete the words

1. s i ng   2. b_n   3. b_g
4. r_ng   5. p_n   6. _ll

Write

ice i _ _   big _ _ _   head _ _ _ _

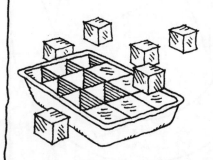  

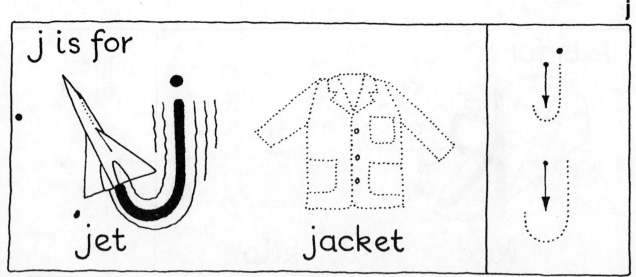

j is for

jet

jacket

Write

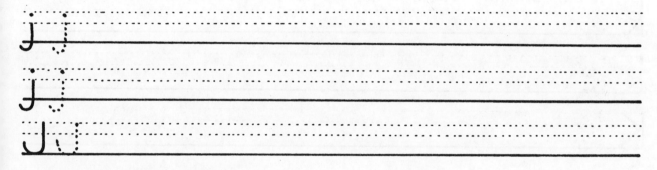

Ring the odd one out

j j j i j j j j   J j J j j j g j
j f J J J J J J   J J J j h j J j

Find the word

jug   _elly   _ar   _et

k

k is for

kite

kilo

Write

k k

k k

K K

Write the words

cake

bike

kick

Jack

Join the dots. Write the word

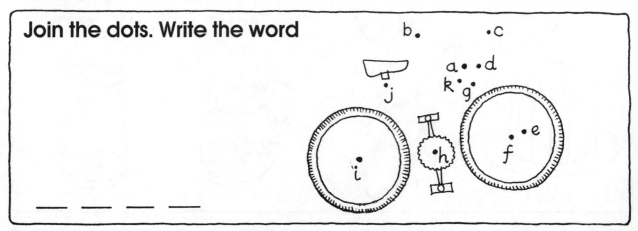

_ _ _ _ _

16

l is for

leg   lemon

Write

l

l

L

Ring the words with l

arm

banana

elephant

lamp

elastic

crocodile

ice-cream

fruit

leg

girl

Make words

lbal   ball   egl _ _ _

nolme _ _ _ _ _   lebl _ _ _ _

a-l practice

Say the letters

E C H K A F I J B G L D

f g i a e l b h d j d j k c

Join the letters

E F G H I J K L

g i j e k l f h

Write

L · i ·

J · j ·

K · k ·

L · l ·

Spell these names

Bill	Jill
Jack	Jeff
Dick	Ali

Listen and do

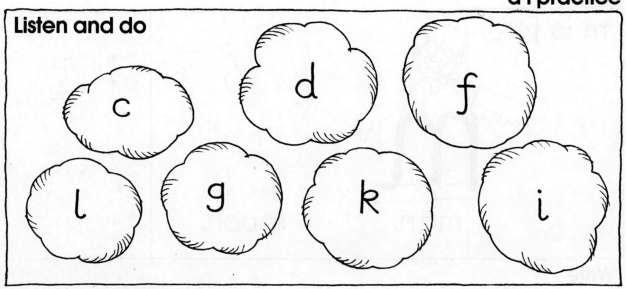

Listen and write

Find and complete

	J			
L	M	P		
	C			
	K			
J	L	L	Y	
	T			

m is for

man   moon

Write

m m

m m

M M

Ring the odd one out

M M M m M   m m M m m

m m m M m   M M M M m

Write our names

Mike   Kim   Jim   Madge

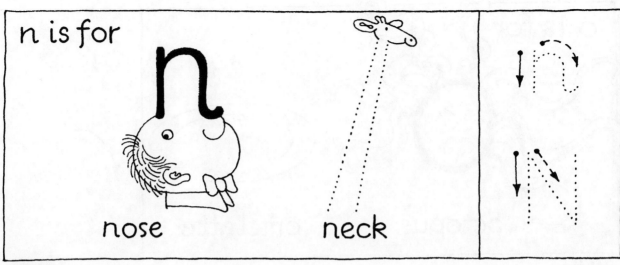

n is for

nose   neck

Write

n n

n n

N N

Join the n's

Write and say

I'm number one

o

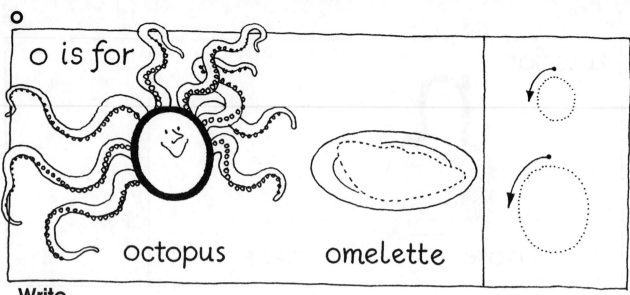

o is for

octopus

omelette

Write

O

O

O

Complete the words

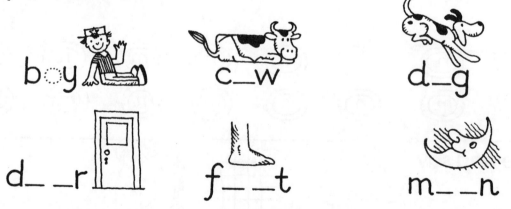

b o y

c_w

d_g

d_ _r

f_ _t

m_ _n

Write and say

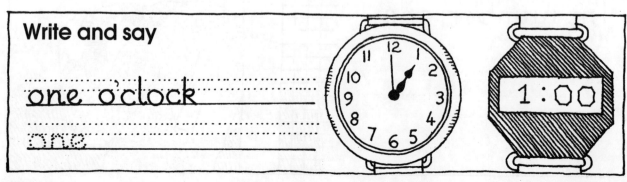

one o'clock

one

22

p is for

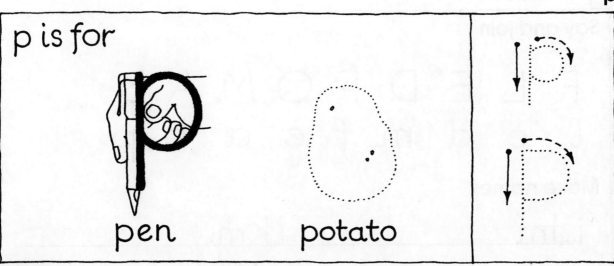

pen   potato

Write

p

p

P

Ring the p's and P's

b d p b P B d F p b g D B P E d p b P b p d

Find and write

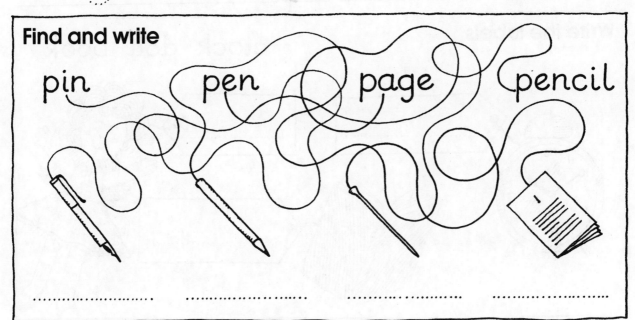

pin   pen   page   pencil

....

a-p practice

Say and join

F L E D P O M A B

l o d m f e a b p

Make names

i Jm   i Km

ne B   e M ki

Write

M   m

N   n

O   o

P   p

Write the labels

clock doll book

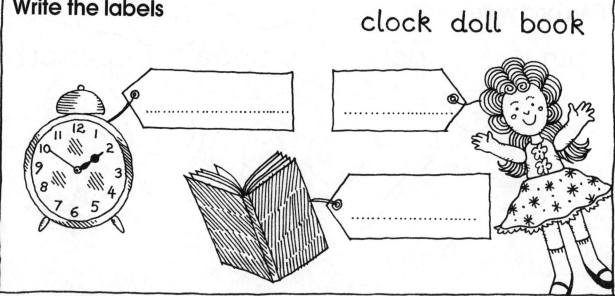

Complete

A B _ D E _ G H _ J K L _ N _ P

Listen and write

Play a game

I spy...

I spy something beginning with...

q is for

question

queen

Write

q ....

q ....

Q ....

Join the q's

p	q	q	p	b	b	q	b	d	q	b	p	p	b	d
q	b	p	q	p	q	b	q	q	b	q	b	d	q	q
b	p	b	b	q	p	p	d	p	d	p	q	q	p	p

Complete

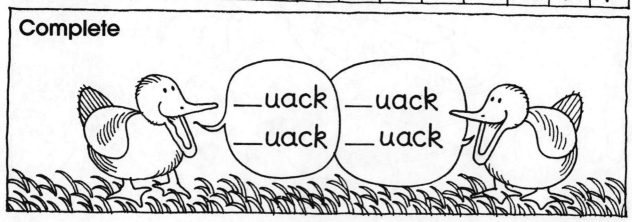

_uack   _uack

_uack   _uack

r is for

robot

rice

Write

r

r

R R

Ring the r's and R's

i e r i o r a e r r i o e r

P K B R P R B K R P P R B P

Colour and write

orange blue red
green brown yellow

[ ] _ _ d

[ ] _ _ u _

[ ] y _ _ _ _ w

[ ] _ _ a _ _ _

[ ] _ _ _ _ e _

[ ] _ _ _ w _

s is for

snake   sock

Write

S s

S s

S s

Complete the words

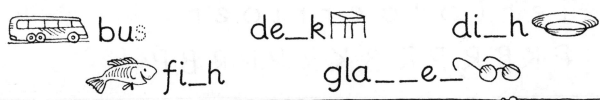

bus   de_k   di_h

fi_h   gla__e_

Do the puzzle

soup

sun

sock   shampoo

sandal

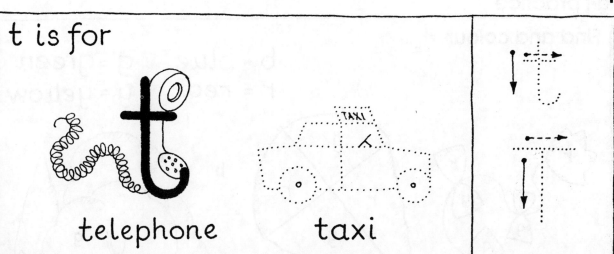

t is for

telephone · taxi

Write

t t

t t

T T

Ring the odd one out

T T (t) T T   t t T t t

T t T T T   t t t T t

Complete and draw

ha_	je_	jacke_	ki_e

a-t practice

Find and colour

b = blue   g = green
r = red   y = yellow

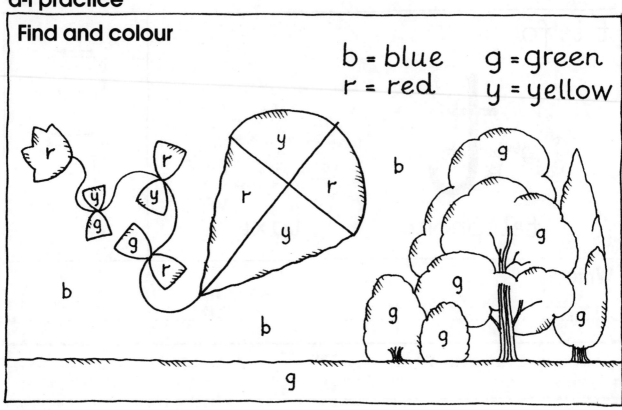

Write

Q   q

R   r

S   s

T   t

Ring the names

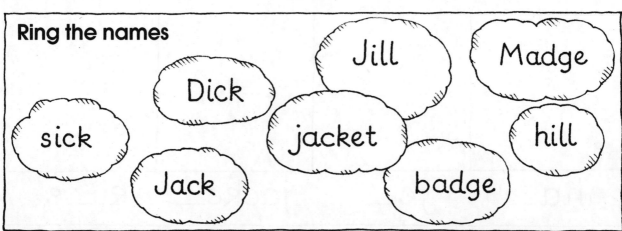

Jill   Madge

Dick

sick   jacket   hill

Jack   badge

38

Listen and do

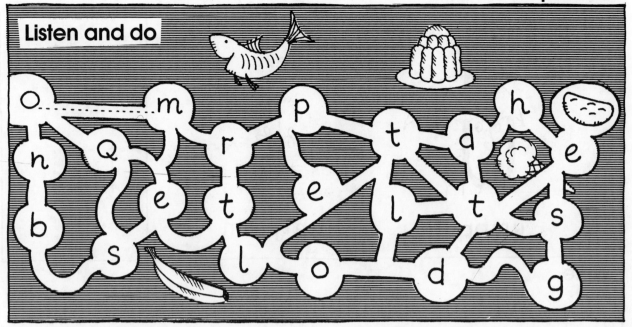

What is it? Write the word

_ _ _ _ _ _ _ _

Make a game

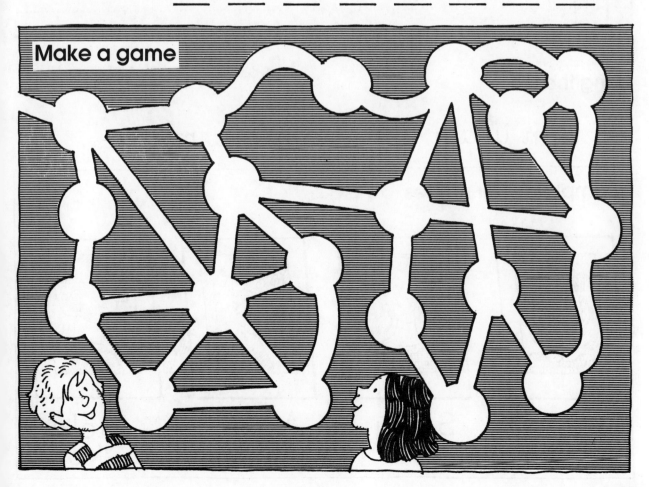

u is for

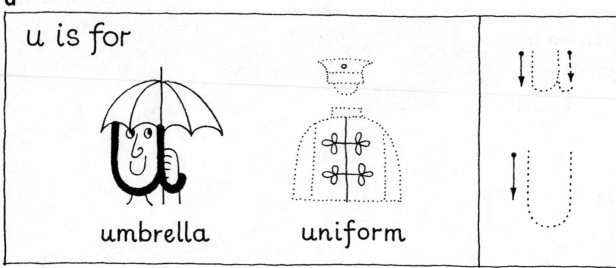

umbrella   uniform

Write

u u

u u

U U

Ring the u's

n m u a n u m u a n n u m a

Complete their names

M u m   S_zy   A_nt   _ncle
                               J_dy   L_ke

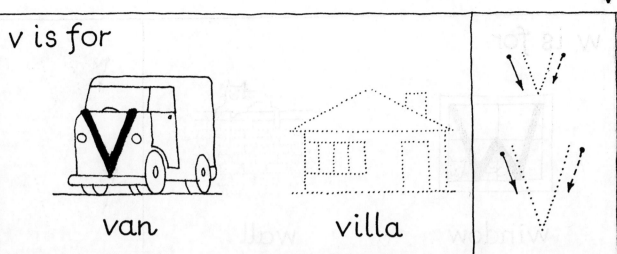

v is for

van   villa

Write

V V

V V

V V

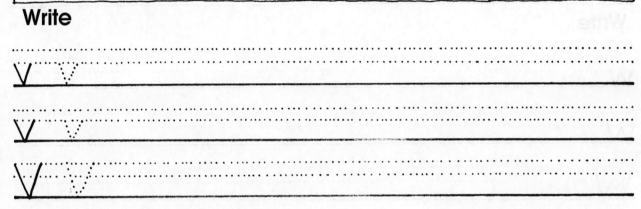

Find and write rhyming words

man sick sock
cat queen old
car leg

quick	van	jar	gold
sick	___	___	___

egg	green	clock	hat
___	___	___	___

w

w is for

window

wall

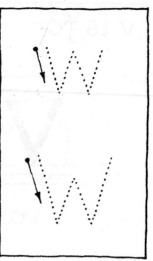

Write

w w

w w

w w

Ring and join the w's

w v v w v w v v v w v w v w

Find and write

wall woman
watch window

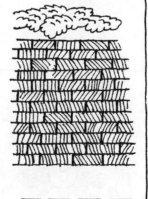

____

42

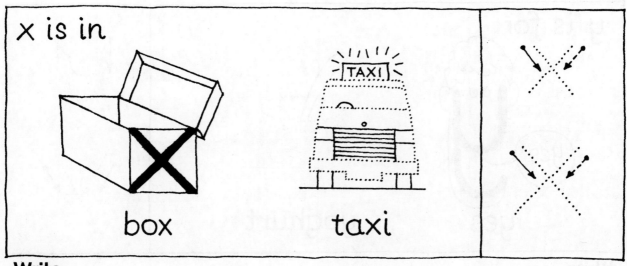

x is in

box   taxi

Write

x x

x x

x x

Colour the x's green. Find the word

x	x	x	a	x	o	t	e	x	l	x	h	x	x	x
x	m	n	o	n	x	i	x	a	b	x	r	o	x	c
x	x	x	l	b	d	x	e	f	a	x	i	k	x	n
x	o	s	t	v	x	w	x	s	u	x	a	e	x	e
x	x	x	m	x	n	o	r	x	e	x	w	v	x	t

Find and write words with x

example

— — —

— — — —

— — — —

y is for

yes

yoghurt

Write

y y

y y

Y Y

Write yes **or** no

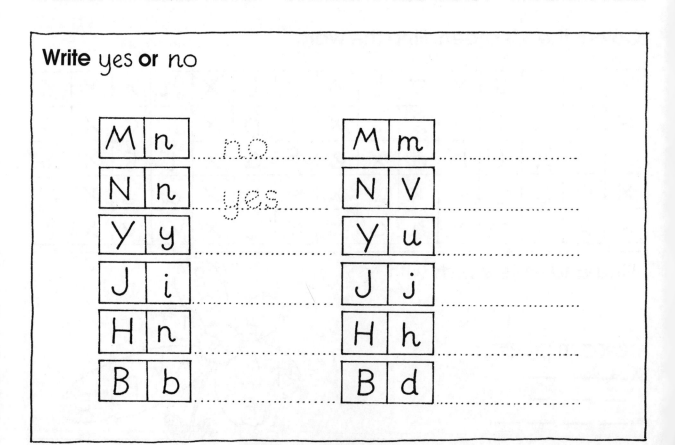

M	n	no	M	m	
N	n	yes	N	V	
Y	y		Y	u	
J	i		J	j	
H	n		H	h	
B	b		B	d	

z is for

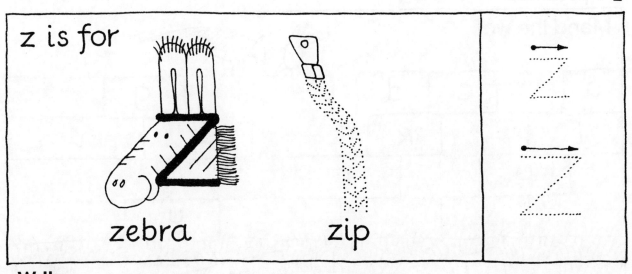

zebra zip

Write

z z

z z

z z

Find and write

moo buzz baa
cock-a-doodle-do zzzz

sheep bee cow cock boy girl

a-z practice

Mend the wall

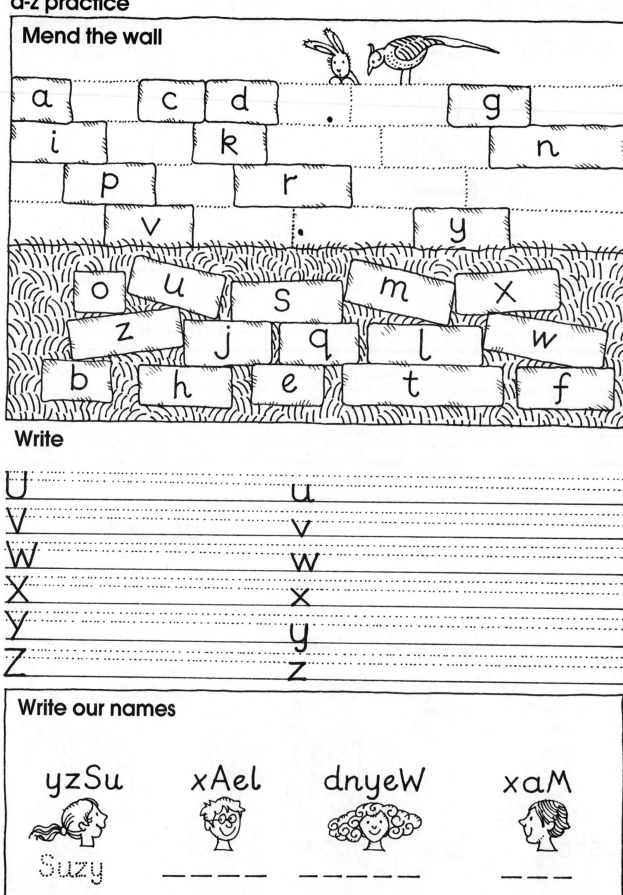

Write

U .... u

V v

W .... w

X x

Y .... y

Z .... z

Write our names

yzSu   xAel   dnyeW   xaM

Suzy   _ _ _ _   _ _ _ _ _   _ _ _

Listen and do

1	2	3	4
– – – –	– – – – – –	– – – – – –	– – – – – –

Find and write the colours

E G N A R O   O L L E Y

D E R O W N E E R G B L U E

Can you find another colour beginning with b ?

....

....
....
....
....
....

numbers 1-3

Tick ☑ if correct

one

one ball	✓
one lamp	
one bag	
one pencil	
one clock	
one key	

one

1

two

two lemons	
two ice-creams	
two eggs	
two jellies	
two cakes	
two jugs	

two

2

three

three boys	
three girls	
three tents	
three jets	
three kites	
three bikes	
three maps	

three

3

Write how many   **numbers 4-6**

four

four	umbrellas	4
	vans	
	windows	
	ants	
	bananas	
	lemons	

four

4

five

five	yoghurts	5
	balls	
	keys	
	elephants	
	cats	

five

5

six

six	arms	6
	legs	
	noses	
	hands	
	fingers	

six

6

49

Write how many

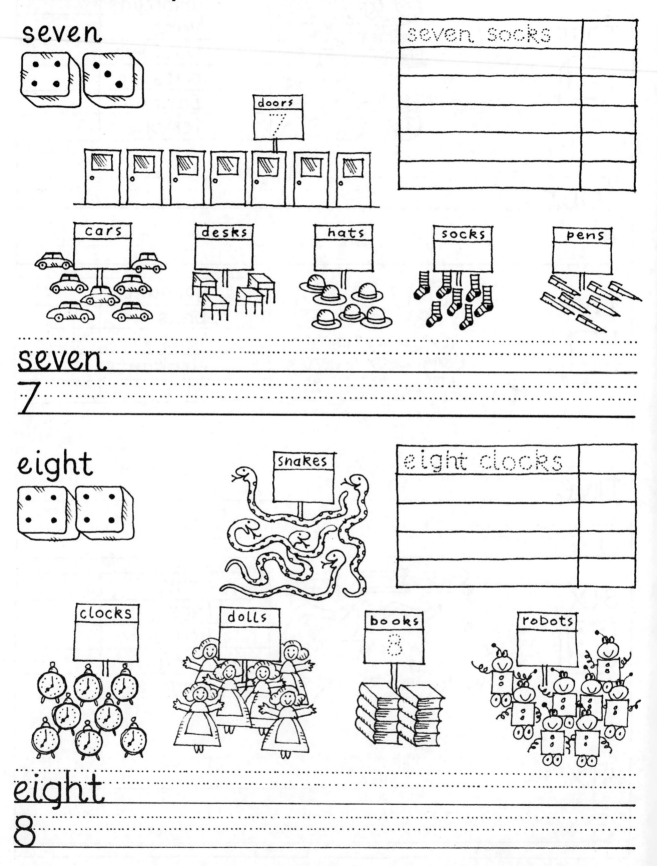

seven

seven socks	

doors 7

cars desks hats socks pens

seven

7

eight

snakes

eight clocks	

clocks dolls books robots

8

eight

8

Count and write

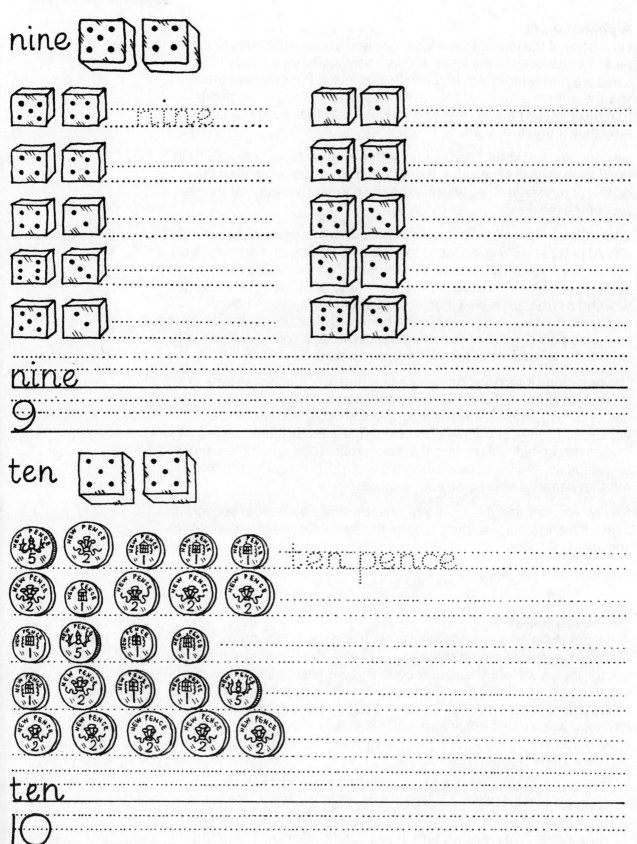

nine

nine

nine

9

ten

ten pence

ten

10

Teacher's notes

Alphabet work

Each page of the alphabet work is organised in the same way. First the pupil is introduced to the letter and its name. Usually two objects or items are presented which begin with that letter. Pupils repeat after you the sentences: *a is for arm, a is for athlete.* Explain to the pupils that most letters have at least two sounds. First, their name. Second, how they sound in a word.

Next, pupils look at the shape of the letter in lower case. They can fill in the dotted shape of the letter. It does not matter too much how they do this at this stage. They will practise the correct formation in the next part of the lesson.

Correct letter formation is shown for both lower and upper case. Pupils should practise writing the letter using the guidelines and arrows given in the book. Demonstrate each stage yourself on the blackboard, pointing out first where to start the letter. Also point out the risers and descenders (the stems which go up and down from the middle guideline). Follow up the work in the book with practice on blank paper or tracing paper, ensuring that the pupils write to a consistent size and height. A full handwriting model is given on page 62.

The next stage is recognition and writing practice. Pupils complete labels, join labels to the correct picture, solve puzzles and play writing games. The main letter already practised will occur and should be written accurately. Letters already covered will also occur and are revised accordingly. Make sure that capitals are used when the word is all in capitals, and lower case when the word is all in lower case. Point out that names always begin with a capital.

Finally, you can use the rhyme or chant in the *Say and do* section on pages 57–61 to practise the sound of the letter. Or you can leave these activities until later.

Cut-out alphabet

A cut-out alphabet is provided in the centre pages. Pupils should colour the letters and then mount these pages on stiff card. They can then cut out the individual letters and numbers. This will give them a complete set of letters in both lower and upper case which they can use in various games and activities. The sets of cards can be kept in an old envelope when not in use. If each set is kept tidy with a rubber band around it, there should not be too many problems. Some ideas for using the cards are suggested below.

1. Pupils play in pairs. They take the same six letters (*A–F, G–L*, etc) from either the lower case or the upper case set of letters. Each pupil shuffles the six letters into a random order. Each pupil then puts a card on the desk in turn. If a card follows another with the same letter, the first pupil to shout the name of the letter wins a

point. The cards are shuffled again and the game carries on. The first pupil to get three points is the winner. This game can be played with the set of numbers as well.

2. Pupils play alone. They take any eight letters from their set and see how many words they can make with the eight letters.

3. Pupils play in pairs. Each pupil chooses a card at random from their partner's set and must identify it. You can play this as a "knock-out" competition. The first pupil in each pair to make three mistakes is eliminated. The winner goes on to play the winner of another pair. You can have several rounds with a semi-final and a final which will produce a class "champion" at the end.

Say and do
Rhymes and chants to reinforce the sounds of each letter appear on pages 57–61. Encourage their use in your pupils' own play outside the classroom and in the playground. Pupils should learn the rhymes and chants by heart. Translate to help with the sense, but do not teach the extra vocabulary and grammar. The rhymes and chants should be learnt simply by their sound and association with the related game or activity. Notes are also provided, suggesting actions or games to accompany each chant.

Revision and practice
Each group of about four letters is followed by revision work and additional practice. Listening exercises come into this area. Notes follow on the revision and practice sections.

a–d Practice (pp 6–7)

Listen and do
Say slowly: *b–d–c–a–c–a–d–b*. Pupils ring the letter heard. Go around and check during the exercise. Repeat as necessary.

Listen and write
Tell the class you are going to spell out a list of names. This means all the words will begin with a capital letter. Spell the following words slowly while pupils write them in their books: *Ada, Dad, Abba*.

Find the letters
Pupils look for the hidden letters and write over them in colour. The hidden letters are: *Aa Bb Cc Dd*.

Say the letters
Pupils try to read each row of letters without help. If necessary they can check back in their books. If there is real difficulty, start to prompt.

Join the letters
Pupils join each upper case letter to the correct lower case in the bottom row.

Write
Pupils practise writing letters without guidance. Go around the class and monitor that the letters are being formed correctly.

Mend the wall
Pupils look at the missing stones. They draw the correct stone in each gap in the wall. The wall should read: *Aa Bb Cc Dd*.

a–h Practice (pp 12–13)
Most of these exercises are similar to those for p 6. See notes for p 6.

Spell these words
Go through the list spelling each word in turn. Pupils follow in their books but they need not repeat. Then let pupils do the same in pairs, correcting each other if possible. You can organise rewards for correct spellings and forfeits for mistakes.

Listen and do
Say slowly: *h–c–e–g–a–d–f–b*. Pupils ring the letter heard. Go around and check during the exercise. Repeat as necessary.

Listen and write
Tell the class you are going to spell out a list in which there is a name. This means one of the words will begin with a capital letter. Spell out the following slowly: head, Heba, badge. See if pupils recognise the name. If not, help them and see if they can change the initial letter to a capital.

Find the letters
This is a picture puzzle with capital letters A to H hidden. Pupils must find them and colour them individually. The easiest way is to draw the outline of each letter in a different colour.

a–l Practice (pp 18–19)
Most of these exercises are similar to those for p 6. See notes for p 6.

Spell these names
Tell the pupils they are going to spell a list of names. Each name begins with a capital letter. Pupils spell each name. Go round the class, then let pupils work in pairs, correcting each other.

Listen and do
Say slowly: *d–l–f–i–k–c–g*. Pupils ring the letter heard. Go around and check during the exercise. Repeat as necessary.

Listen and write
Tell the class you are going to spell out a list in which there is a name. This means one of the words will begin with a capital leter. Spell out the following slowly: *ball, Bill, bike, cake*. See if pupils recognise the name. If not, help them and see if they can change the initial letter to a capital.

Find and complete
Tell pupils to complete this crossword in capital letters. They should look through their books to find the words, all of which are known. The solution to the crossword is as follows: **down** jacket **across** lamp, jelly.

54

a–p Practice (pp 24–25)

Make names
The mixed up names are: *Jim, Ben, Kim, Mike*.

The trick in each case is for the pupil to remember to find and begin with the capital letter.

Write the labels
The labels are: *clock, doll, book*. They can be either in upper or lower case but, in either case, all the letters should be the same (that is, no initial capital).

Complete
Pupils fill in the missing letters from the alphabet so far covered:
C–F–I–M–O.

Listen and write
Spell out the following words: *name, moon, map, man*. Pupils write them in their books. Point out first that there are no names in this list.

Play a game: I-spy
Pupils study the picture for items beginning with any letter that you identify. Say: *I spy something beginning with . . . (X)*. Pupils find any item beginning with that letter. The one who finds it first can carry on the game with another letter using the same *I spy . . .* formula. Pupils can also play this game in pairs.

a–t Practice (pp 38–39)

Find and colour
Pupils colour the picture with blue for the areas marked *b*, green for the areas marked *g*, yellow for the areas marked *y*, and red, for the areas marked *r*.

Ring the names
Pupils ring the names only, identifying them by their capital letters. The names are: *Dick, Jill, Madge, Jack*.

Listen and do
Explain that you are going to spell out something to eat. Pupils must trace the word through the maze. If they do this correctly, they will find a clue to the food at the end. Spell out the word: *omelette*. Pupils then write out the word below.

Make a game
Pupils use the empty maze to hide a word of their own choice. This is best done by writing the word in sequence through the maze and then filling in all the other blanks with letters at random. They can tell their partner it's something to eat, or an animal, or something in the classroom. The partner must try to find the item.

a–z Practice (pp 46–47)

Mend the wall
Pupils look at the missing stones. They draw the correct stone in each gap in the wall. The wall should read: *abcdefghijklmnopqrstuvwxyz*.

Write our names
The correct names are: *Suzy, Alex, Wendy, Max*. As before, pupils should begin with the capital letter in each name.

Listen and do
Spell out each animal's name: *ant, elephant, octopus, crocodile*. All of these are known from the book and can be found in it. Pupils write the name, identify the animal and draw it.

Find and write the colours
There are five colours radiating from the circle, and one colour hidden in the circle. Pupils find them and colour the segments of the circle the correct colour. The five radiating colours are: *blue, red, orange, yellow, green*. The first or last letters of these make the secret colour: *brown*. Pupils write this in the speech bubble and colour the ring brown.

Numbers
Numbers one to ten are introduced at the end of the course. Practice is provided in forming figures and words. Use the exercises to reinforce and revise.

Tick if correct
Pupils count each group and if the number corresponds to that in the list, put a tick. Otherwise put a cross.

Write how many
Pupils count the items in each group and write the correct number, in words, in front of the word in the list. A box is supplied at the end of each line for pupils to write the number in figures. On page 50 pupils can also write the correct number on the signposts.

Exercises on page 50 require the pupil to write the word for the item as well.

Count and write
This exercise adds some simple arithmetic to the task. The total is written in words. The correct totals are: *nine, eight, six, nine, seven, two, nine, eight, five, nine*.

In the second sentence, the answers are: *ten pence, nine pence, eight pence, ten pence, ten pence*.

Say and do

Page	Letter	Rhyme and Notes

2 a

A is for alphabet. A–B–C.
D–E–F and G.

Clap together to a four-beat line, clapping on the stress marks.
There is a slight pause between *D–E–F*.

3 b

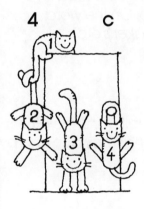

Bag beats bat.
Bat beats ball.
Ball beats bag.

This is a game like 'Stone, scissors, paper'. Each item is
represented by a different hand shape. Pupils play in pairs. They
put out their hands simultaneously in any one of the three shapes,
saying the word at the same time. One of the shapes 'wins' over
the other. *Bat* wins over *ball*. *Ball* wins over *bag*. *Bag* wins over *bat*.
If both say the same word, they repeat.

4 c

One, two, three, four.
Count the cats on the door.

Draw a simple picture on the board of four cats doing acrobatics
on a door. Number them 1 to 4 in figures. Pupils point to and count
the cats as they chant.

5 d

This is the doctor's
desk/door/dog/dish.

Pupils point to each picture at the bottom of page 5 in turn, saying
This is the doctor's dish/dog/door/desk etc. You can add to the list
with other *d*-words as they are learnt.

8 e

Hello, echo, echo, echo.
It's me, me, me.

This chant works like a 'round'. Put four pupils facing into different
corners of the classroom, calling through cupped hands. As Pupil
One finishes the first line of the chant, Pupil Two starts, and so on.
Let each pupil say the chant three or four times continuously. This
should produce a good echo effect at the end as each pupil
finishes in turn.

Page	Letter	Rhyme and Notes

9   **f**

Find a fish.
Make a wish.

This is a 'magic chant' to be said when each pupil finds the fish in the picture on page 9. After saying it, they can make a silent wish.

10   **g**

Grow grow green grass.

An activity chant. Pupils stand in a ring in groups of 3 or 4. They pile their hands alternatively on top of each other in the centre of the ring. Then they chant together. As they say ... *grow*, the person whose hand is on the bottom of the pile moves it to the top. The idea is to go faster and faster. Pupils can end up saying *grow, grow,* ... as fast as they can.

11   **h**

Hop, hop, hop to the butcher's shop
and when you get there – stop!

A hopping game. Demonstrate in the classroom and let pupils play it in the playground. While you are hopping, the idea is to mime the person whose shop you are going to. On the word ... *stop*, land on both feet. Add other shops (*baker's* etc).

14   **i**

Ice-cream, ice-cream.
I scream for ice-cream.

Explain the play on words in this chant. One pupil starts, the others join in one by one. They can clap while chanting. They can end by saying *We all scream for ice-cream.*

15   **j**

Jacket and jeans, jacket and jeans.
Pockets full of jelly-beans.

A skipping game for the playground.

16   **k**

I'm the king of the castle,
keeper of the keys.

A chant to show that you are the winner, the first to finish something or the one on top *eg* the first to climb something. Explain its use and suggest opportunities for using it. Do your pupils have any chants of their own which they use in the same way?

Page	Letter	Rhyme and Notes

17   **l**

She's still in bed. She isn't ill.
Lazy, lazy, lazy Jill.

Accompany this chant with wagging of fingers. It is a 'ticking off' chant. It can be acted out with one person playing Jill and another her mother or father. For boys, use *he* instead of *she* and change the name to *Bill*.

20   **m**

Man in the moon, man in the moon.
Make me rich and make it soon.

Chant together, clapping on stress marks. A four-beat line.

21   **n**

No nuts, no nuts, no, not one.
Niddle-noddle, niddle-noddle, now we're done.

This is a choosing chant for starting a game. Pupils stand in a ring. One pupil chants, pointing to a different pupil on each word. The pupil who is pointed at on the word *done* is chosen. English children say *You're it.*

22   **o**

Open, open, open, open,
open, open, open the door.

Pupils start with both arms stretched out in front of them. As they chant, they slowly open their arms until they are stretched out sideways. They can go back to the original position chanting *Shut the door* in the same way.

23   **p**

Pass the pencil, pretty Polly, please.

A tongue-twister. The idea is to say it as quickly as possible. Explain that *pretty Polly* is a popular name for a tame parrot.

26   **q**

Quick, quick, the queen is sick.

A mini-drama in which one pupil pretends to be the queen ruling over everyone else. The queen then pretends suddenly to be ill. The others all chant together.

35   **r**

Red lorry, yellow lorry.

A tongue-twister which can be quite hard to say quickly. Draw a simple picture on the board of two lorries. Pupils copy the picture, and colour the two lorries, one red, one yellow.

Page	Letter	Rhyme and Notes

36   **s**   *Spinner, spin, spin, spin.*
Spinner, stop!

This is a measuring chant when you are playing spinner games, usually in pairs. The pupil who is controlling says the chant repeating *spin, spin spin* until s/he wants the other to stop. Then s/he says *Spinner, stop!*

37   **t**   *Ten little taxis waiting in a line.*
One drives off and then there are nine.

Line up ten pupils and let them all chant the first line together. You say the second line, and the pupil at the top of the line drives off. You can continue until there are none left. Here are some suggested words:

Ten little taxis waiting in a line,
One drives off and then there are nine.
Nine little taxis waiting by a gate,
One drives off and then there are eight.
Eight little taxis waiting in Devon,
One drives off and then there are seven.
Seven little taxis waiting at the pics,
One drives off and there there are six.
Six little taxis waiting by a hive,
One drives off and then there are five.
Five little taxis waiting at the door,
One drives off and then there are four.
Four little taxis waiting by a tree,
One drives off and then there are three.
Three little taxis waiting at the zoo,
One drives off and then there are two.
Two little taxis waiting in the sun,
One drives off and then there is one.
One little taxi waiting all alone,
One drives off and then there are none

40   **u**   *Umbrella, up, up, up.*

Pupils mime raising an umbrella as they say *up, up, up.* You can lower the umbrella in the same way by saying *Umbrella down, down, down.*

Page	Letter	Rhyme and Notes

41   **v**

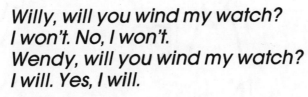

Vera is vain.
Vera is very vain.

A 'round the class' game. You start by saying *Vera is vain*. Each pupil in turn repeats, adding one extra *very*. The last *very* in each case is stressed heavily. Pupils must keep count of the number of *very's*. Limit this to what the pupils can realistically do, perhaps five or six.

42   **w**

Willy, will you wind my watch?
I won't. No, I won't.
Wendy, will you wind my watch?
I will. Yes, I will.

A mini-dialogue to be acted out with three pupils. Make sure the intonation and stress is quite heightened. Different groups can 'audition' to see which group acts the best. The whole class or a 'panel of judges' can give points.

43   **x**

Fox!
Rabbit!
Bang!

A game. Divide the class in half any way you like (boys and girls, down the middle, back and front). One half are foxes, the other half are rabbits. All the class stands up. You shout *Fox!* and the last rabbit to sit down is out. Any fox who sits down is also out. You shout *Rabbit!* and anyone at all who sits down is out. You shout *Bang!* and both groups must sit down. The last one in either group to sit down is out. Once they have got the idea, pupils can take turns to do the calling out.

44   **y**

Yoghurt. Yum-yum!

Explain that *yum-yum* is what English children say when something tastes good. Rub your tummy and say *Yoghurt, yum-yum* to show that you like yoghurt. Let each pupil do the same, naming a food that they like.

45   **z**

Bee. Buzz-buzz!

Name an animal or an insect and let the class make the noise that the animal or insect makes. You can add dog (*woof-woof*), cat (*miaow*), bird (*tweet-tweet*), donkey (*eeyore*). It will be interesting to compare these English sounds with animal sounds in the pupils' own language.